Original title:
The Path of the Pothos

Copyright © 2025 Creative Arts Management OÜ
All rights reserved.

Author: Lila Davenport
ISBN HARDBACK: 978-1-80581-865-6
ISBN PAPERBACK: 978-1-80581-392-7
ISBN EBOOK: 978-1-80581-865-6

Harmony in Leafy Labyrinths

In a jungle of green, they twist and cheer,
Leaves whisper secrets to vines far and near.
A party of stems, with a drink made of dew,
Dancing in sunlight, all dressed up in hue.

Giggles erupt from the root-bound crew,
'Who needs a garden? We're thriving anew!
A leaf here, a tendril there, oh what a sight!
In leafy labyrinths, everything feels right.

Nurtured by Sunlight's Caress

Basking in rays, the leaves have a chat,
'Is that a sunbeam? Let's welcome it back!'
They stretch and they giggle, a photosynth cheer,
While avoiding the shadow, they simply don't fear.

They play peek-a-boo with a curious bug,
"Hey there!" they laugh, "Join us for a hug!"
Warmth wraps around them, a cozy embrace,
In the dance of the day, they find their own space.

Flourish in the Silent Shade

In the quiet of shade, the vines get a break,
They sip on cool air while others are baked.
'No sunburn for us!' they all chant with glee,
'Just us and the silence, feel the chill, whee!'

Little green spirits float in the still,
Imagining sunlight, they pine for the thrill.
But a sloth in the corner, oh so serene,
Reminds them that chill can also be keen.

Legends of an Ambitious Climber

Once there was a vine, with goals to achieve,
Aspirations so high, it could hardly believe.
"Let's scale that tall trellis, a kingdom to claim!
With courage and leaves, I'll have my own fame!"

With every inch gained, the crowd would all cheer,
"Look at it go! It's the climber we revere!"
A show-off at heart, but with roots in good fun,
This legend of green laughs under the sun.

The Language of Verdant Trails

In the jungle of green, things twist and shout,
Leaves do the salsa, no doubt about.

The roots gossip softly, sharing their tales,
Of parties by moonlight, and wind-dancing gales.

A leaf winks at a bug, saying, 'Join the fun!'
While a sneaky little vine plots a prank on the sun.

In this lively garden, the laughter is real,
As plants swap their secrets, making each other squeal.

Whispering Vines and Hidden Hues

Vines whisper stories, tangled and sly,
About hidden rainbows that pass by the eye.

With shades of green, they play peek-a-boo,
Winking at passersby, painting skies blue.

The petals are prim, but the stems tell a joke,
As sunlight tickles them, they giggle and poke.

Nature's comedians, each leaf shines with flair,
Creating a spectacle, charmingly rare.

The Way of the Emerald Climber

Emerald climbers, reaching for the sky,
Tell jokes to the clouds, oh so sly.

With each little tendril, they wave and flirt,
While the ladybugs dance in their coats of dirt.

Growing upwards with glee, they make such a scene,
A green comedy show, painted vividly sheen.

At dusk, they gather, under starry displays,
Cracking up the crickets in amusing arrays.

Tapestry Woven with Nature's Thread

In a tapestry bright, nature's humor weaves,
Palms giggle and sway, like laughing leaves.

A bloom's bright blush, a cheeky surprise,
While daisies chime in, with twinkling eyes.

Grass tickles toes as it whispers and sways,
Crafting hilarious tales in the sun's golden rays.

From roots to the sky, they paint a bright fable,
In this whimsical garden, joy's truly stable.

Echoes in the Leafy Labyrinth

In a tangle of green, I lost my shoe,
A vine whispered, "Come play, I dare you!"
Chasing shadows, I stumbled on a gnome,
Who told me to water the ferns at home.

Laughter erupted from a cactus near,
"Don't poke fun! I don't bite, I just spear!"
The ferns rolled their leaves, in rhythmic dance,
While I tried to figure out my stance.

A parrot squawked, "Can you hear the glee?"
Turns out it was just a bad melody!
With each twist and turn, I bumped and swayed,
This leafy maze was where pranks were played.

So if you wander where greens entangle,
Beware of the fun, the mischief will wrangle!
The laughter may come from a leafy friend,
In this chaotic jungle, the jokes won't end.

Silence of the Clinging Shadows

In a corner with creepers, the shadows blend,
Whispers of mischief, around each bend.
A squirrel critiqued my choice of snack,
"Yogurt again? You really need a snack attack!"

The vines laughed softly, what a curious sight,
They tangled and wrangled till the dawn's light.
One sage leaf said, "What's the fuss all about?"
"Life's a garden party! Join in, no doubt!"

But there was a snail, who was stuck in a dream,
"I'm winning this race!" He said with a gleam.
While thoughts of the finish line floated about,
His pace was so slow, he forgot to come out!

So here in these shadows, the echoes resound,
A tapestry woven with laughter all around.
Join us with giggles, take your mind for a spin,
And dance with the plants as the joy starts to win.

Tendrils of Green Whisper

In corners they dance, a wiggly spree,
These little green vines, so wild and free.
Climbing the curtains, oh what a sight,
Who needs a ladder? They'll take flight!

With sneaky intent, they twist and they twine,
Chasing the sunlight, sipping on brine.
Watch out, dear cat, they're on the attack,
A jungle adventure, they've got no lack!

Journey Through Leafy Veins

With each little leaf, a tale to unfold,
Of travels and triumphs, of daring and bold.
A vine on a mission, so quirky and spry,
Eavesdropping on plants, oh me, oh my!

Swinging through spaces, they giggle and sway,
Searching for snacks, what's on the buffet?
A feast of sunbeams, a banquet of cheer,
These mischievous greens, the party's right here!

Shadows of a Climbing Heart

A heart full of hope, tangled in green,
Chasing the light, a curious scene.
With every new leaf, they shout, 'Look at me!'
A climbing romance, oh, can you see?

Twisting and turning, they play hide and seek,
Flirting with florals, they're never weak.
"Oh dear," they whisper, "Is it time to grow?"
And off they go dancing, with quite the show!

Serenity in Silken Vines

In a world of chaos, these vines find their peace,
Drifting through rooms, their worries do cease.
They bask in the calm, like yoga on leaves,
Unraveling stress, while the whole world grieves.

With whispers of laughter and gentle surprise,
They sip on the sunlight, with twinkling eyes.
Winding in circles, creating their nest,
Serenity found, and they know they're blessed!

Graceful Wanderings

In a jungle of green and vines,
The leaf dances like silly signs.
Step over that rock, avoid the mud,
Oops, fell down—look! There's a puddle flood.

Frogs giggle from their leafy thrones,
While I trip over my shoe's bright tones.
Swinging arms, I sway with glee,
A true acrobat—can't you see?

The Echoes of Growth

Once a sprout, I aimed for the top,
Daily I climbed, couldn't make it stop.
Look at me now, I'm tall and proud,
But find me down here, lost in my shroud.

I whispered to leaves in the shade,
They tickled my sides, how I swayed.
A chattering buddy will always be,
With vines so clever, who needs a spree?

Verdant Dreams Unfurled

With each curl, I make a new friend,
Swinging 'round corners, the fun won't end.
A leaf wave here, a stalk there,
Who knew a plant could dance with flair?

I tell jokes to the soil below,
It cracks up hard, can't help but show.
Roots tickle and wiggle with delight,
They cheer for my dreams, oh what a sight!

Climbing Higher

Reaching for sun, I stretch and shout,
A little bird chirps, full of doubt.
"You're too ambitious, slow your pace!"
I laugh, and keep on my leafy race.

On the fence, I peek and gawk,
Is that a squirrel? Time for a talk!
He quips back, so bright and spry,
In my world of green, we can both fly.

Breathing Deeper

With each breath, I grow and sway,
Taking in sunshine, hip-hip-hooray!
Every blunder, a giggle I seek,
Sprouting joy; growing a tweak.

A breeze passes, like whispers near,
I twirl 'round, no room for fear.
Who knew being green could be such fun?
Laughing and growing under the sun!

The Luminous Journey

With leaves so bright, they dance and sway,
A journey begins, come what may.
In every corner, they seek a light,
Finding joy in the day and the night.

Each twist and turn, a secret shared,
Through rooms where laughter once dared.
They stretch their vines, a playful trick,
Daring us to pick them quick.

They whisper tales of where they've been,
Around old books and dusty sheen.
A comedy in every crevice around,
In the garden of life, they're renowned.

So here they twirl, with glee and grace,
Turning life's clutter into a race.
In a pot or a hanging rack,
These little comedians never look back.

Swaying in the Afternoon Glow

In the sun's warm hug, they giggle and play,
As if they know it's the best kind of day.
They sway with gusto, in breezy delight,
Making shadows dance, what a silly sight!

A friend once said, 'Do they ever stop?'
But they respond with a wiggle and plop.
They tease the sun, with a bashful grin,
Creating chaos as they twirl and spin.

With every inch, they claim their space,
In the world's great show, they embrace the race.
Roots tickle softly in the earth below,
While leaves above put on their show.

They gather dust yet shine so bright,
With quirky quirks, life feels just right.
In a whimsy waltz, they steal the light,
Swaying boldly, heartily, through the night.

Veins of Memory

In green and gold, the tales are spun,
Each vein a journey, layered fun.
They bask in echoes of laughter past,
Holding on tightly, as friendships last.

With every curl, a story told,
Of rainy days and sunshine bold.
They weave through echoes, subtle and sly,
In the heart's tangled web, they fly high.

Each leaf a page in a hefty tome,
Reminding us all, we're never alone.
They drink from the cup of sunlight bright,
Dancing through shadows into the night.

A pot of mischief, a loyal friend,
With vines that stretch and never bend.
In the tapestry of time, they're the mix,
Crafting memories with clever tricks.

Winding Through Forgotten Spaces

In corners hidden, they plot their fun,
With tiny whispers, they tease the sun.
A little misadventure, they orchestrate,
Unraveling stories, they celebrate.

Crawling past shoes and old dusty books,
Each twist brings laughter with a few funny looks.
They're the uninvited guests at tea,
Who spill the sugar and giggle with glee.

Among the cobwebs, they throw a dance,
Awakening shadows, giving them a chance.
They bloom in chaos, unfurl with flair,
Scattering joy in the stagnant air.

So here they wind, with a sense of cheer,
Through dusty spaces, they persevere.
In forgotten nooks, they make their claim,
In the comedy of life, they steal the fame.

In the Heart of the Jungle

In the heart where vines entwine,
Lies a creature so divine.
It wiggles with a funny grace,
Dancing leaves in leafy space.

Lizards laugh as they peek through,
Wondering what this plant will do.
With every twist, it takes a dive,
Maybe it just wants to thrive!

Mischievous roots stretch all about,
Like they're trying to figure out,
Which way's up, which way is down,
In this ever-swirling crown.

Jungle vibes are never bland,
As this greenery makes its stand.
Giggling in the humid air,
What a lucky vine, I swear!

Secrets of the Climbing Jewel

A jewel with leaves, oh so green,
Climbing high, it's quite the scene.
Whispers in the morning light,
Tickling trees with all its might.

Gather 'round, the critters say,
This plant is here to save the day!
With roots that tickle and leaves that sway,
It offers shade in a funny way.

What secrets does it wrap so tight?
Perhaps it dreams of flight at night.
Each curl a story, every twist a tale,
Of slipping trunks and leaves that sail.

In a world where rocks must yield,
This climbing jewel claims the field.
A laugh, a curl, a twist of fate,
In nature's dance, it celebrates!

Tapestry of Leaf and Light

Weaving threads of sun and shade,
A tapestry that's never made.
Leaves are laughing up above,
Swirling hints of clever love.

Light beams tumble through each fold,
As the green stories unfold.
It's a party in the plants,
Where even branches do a dance!

With tiny bugs in vibrant hues,
Joining in with funny moves.
Wiggling leaves and wobbly vines,
Creating jokes in bright designs.

Sunshine's artist, shadows play,
Crafting dreams throughout the day.
In this canvas, life's a song,
Where every twist just feels so wrong!

Resilience Amongst Ruins

Amidst the stones where shadows creep,
A leafy hero starts to leap.
With roots that giggle, leaves that cheer,
It whispers secrets loud and clear.

Once lost in rubble, dust, and grime,
It laughs at fate, it laughs at time.
Growing tall against the odds,
Resilience is the best of gods!

With each wise crack and silly smile,
This plant defies each heavy trial.
Stone may crumble, skies may weep,
But in its joy, the earth will sleep!

So here's a toast to leafy friends,
In wild places where laughter blends.
With roots that dance and leaves that sway,
Life's a giggle, come what may!

Echoes of a Garden's Embrace

In a corner, vines take flight,
Whispering secrets, tangled tight.
They giggle as they twist and twine,
Playing hide and seek, quite divine.

A leaf sneezed, and oh, what a ruckus,
Stirred the soil to join the circus.
Squirrels laughed, the sun turned red,
While shadows danced and flowers bled.

The worms in suits held a parade,
In bedrock splendor, charms displayed.
With roots so deep, humor so spry,
A party hosted, oh my, oh my!

Yet the pots were jealous of the show,
With plans to steal the spotlight's glow.
A dance-off happened, roots entwined,
Now who's the king? Who's left behind?

Climbing Towards the Sun

A daring sprout with dreams so grand,
Claimed the fence, gave it a hand.
"Up, up, I'll go!" it proudly sighed,
While neighbors watched, eyes open wide.

The clouds chuckled, rain clouds did weep,
"What's this ruckus? Want to leap?"
The bird flew down, gave advice,
"Don't aim too high, or think twice!"

A butterfly twirled, critiqued the flair,
"Your leaves look fine, your roots don't care!"
But still that sprout, with heart so bold,
Took the stage, worth their weight in gold.

Through tangled laughs and sunny skies,
Its journey sparked, yet more surprise.
Blurred lines between fun and flight,
Each climb a giggle, pure delight.

Spirals of Growth and Grace

In the garden, laughter swirls,
With twisted vines that dance and twirl.
A caterpillar showed up late,
Bringing stories of strange fate.

"Hey, listen up! I found my groove!"
Said the flower, in a vivid move.
While snails composed a slow parade,
Their homes adorned, sweet serenade.

The fronds all shared a wise debate,
Is it fate or just chance that's great?
With every twist, they joked and pranced,
Nature's rhythm, a merry dance.

And as the sun began to fade,
The leaves were lit, like a glade.
In spirals round, they wrapped in jest,
A waltz of growth, they all were blessed.

Secrets of the Lush Canopy

High above, the branches scheme,
In whispered tones, they plot and dream.
"Who will steal the sunshine today?"
Chattered leaves in a leafy fray.

Among the greens, a raccoon peeped,
"I found the stash, while you all slept!"
With cheeks so full, it dashed away,
Leaving laughter in bright array.

An owl hooted, wisdom unspun,
"Don't lose your head, just have some fun!"
And down below, a critter raced,
To snag the shine and claim first place.

So sing the trees of what they know,
With roots entwined, in a grand show.
In canopies where secrets bask,
Life unravels, no need to ask.

The Color of Growth

In a corner, green and bright,
A plant takes on a daring flight.
With leaves so large, they block the sun,
Saying, "Hey there, look at me, I'm fun!"

Pothos dreams of grander things,
Like climbing high on sylvan wings.
But tangled up in all that mess,
He grins and thinks, "I'm still the best!"

Growing fast, he hops around,
In pots where laughter can be found.
With every twist, he shares a joke,
In leafy whispers when you poke.

A splash of green, a smile anew,
In every room, he paints the view.
With humor thick and roots that roam,
Our leafy friend has made a home!

Tango with the Tangles

In the living room, a dance begins,
With leaves that wriggle, twist, and spin.
A tango here, a cha-cha there,
Pothos pirouettes without a care.

He finds some wires, he thinks, 'Ooh fun!'
And there he goes, 'Let's dance, everyone!'
With every step, he's lost in grace,
A vine that dreams of outer space.

He twirls around the lamp so bright,
And says, 'Excuse me, I'm taking flight!'
With a flick of green, he claims the room,
Twisting the gloom into joyous bloom.

No partners needed, he dances alone,
A joyful rebel in his leafy throne.
In the midst of all this leafy glee,
He whispers, 'Let's live a dancing spree!'

Whispers Among the Vines

In the still of night, soft secrets bloom,
Among the vines that wiggle and loom.
A joke shared here, a giggle there,
Pothos laughs without a care.

Each leaf a ear, each stem a friend,
They plot and scheme, the fun won't end.
In every nook, they spin a tale,
Of grand adventures and leafy trails.

"Did you hear the one of the sun?"
Said a leaf, "It thought it was number one!"
Giggling softly, they hold their breath,
As shadows dance in their leafy nest.

With roots entwined, they share their dreams,
In a world bursting at the seams.
Among the vines, where whispers roam,
Pothos declares, "You're never alone!"

Through Trellis and Time

In the garden, a race begins,
With leafy friends and cheeky grins.
Pothos climbs through tangled frames,
Believing he's won all the games.

With every twist, a story flows,
Of tangled paths and plant-like prose.
"Look at me! I'm king of green!"
He shouts aloud, a leafy scene.

Each knot a laugh, each leaf a cheer,
As time goes by, they thrive right here.
With sunlight spilling all around,
In leafy laughter, joy is found.

Through trellis high and roots so low,
Pothos reigns where fun will grow.
In quirky twists of fate and time,
He plants his joys in leafy rhyme!

Journey Through Lush Shadows

In a jungle of leaves, I must tread,
With ivy on my shoes, I feel misled.
The lizards watch me, and they laugh with glee,
While I trip on branches, as clumsy as can be.

My hat flies off, a bird makes a nest,
I wave goodbye; it'll be their new quest.
The shadows tease me, they play peekaboo,
I stumble and tumble, oh, what a view!

The air is thick, like pudding in the sky,
With every step I take, my sneakers sigh.
The sunlight flickers, like a dance in the breeze,
As I awkwardly swerve, trying to catch my knees.

Yet amidst the chaos, I grin and giggle,
These emerald giants make my heart wiggle.
For each little mishap, I find some delight,
In this wild adventure, everything feels right.

A Climb to Solitude

Up I climb, the vines they beckon,
Though my balance is poor, I have no second.
The ground below seems much too far,
As I swing like Tarzan without a car.

A squirrel shouts, "Hey, move over there!"
I nearly slip, cause his stare is a glare.
With every step up, I might lose my hat,
This journey of mine is a bit like a bat.

But the view at the top, oh what a tease,
The clouds are now friends; they dance with the breeze.
I giggle aloud, no one's around me,
Just a lumpy rock and a begging bee.

I sit on a ledge, the world seems to spin,
While pondering why I climbed up this fin.
Nature's my partner, and we share this fun,
In this comedy show, I'm the only one!

Embracing Nature's Embrace

Wrapped in green, I start to sway,
But the leaves are tickling; I push them away.
Nature hugs tight with her leafy hand,
While I trip on roots, just like she planned.

A butterfly lands on my nose for a rest,
I sneeze it off, feeling far from the best.
With nature's cheer, I slip on some dew,
It's slippery here, like walking on goo!

The trees are giggling, their branches a-shake,
"Be careful, dear friend, don't make a great quake!"
I grin at the birds, they cackle a tune,
While I juggle my snacks under a cartoon moon.

Embracing this chaos, I feel quite alive,
Though I tumble and stumble, I still manage to thrive.
Each rustle and laugh brings a smile to my face,
In this wacky affair, I find my grace.

Curves of Green Serenity

Winding paths twist like a confused snake,
I wish I had thought, for goodness' sake!
With branches that bow, and weeds that fight,
I shuffle along, a comical sight.

A ladybug rolls, spins twice in the air,
While I'm tangled in vines, without a care.
Moss cushions my fall as I trip on my feet,
The forest erupts in laughter, so sweet!

A creek nearby bubbles, a laugh in the flow,
As I make a splash, with a loud "Whoa!"
With my shoes now squishy, and socks full of glee,
I'm the jester of nature, just wait and see!

Yet amidst the giggles, I find some peace,
In the curves of green, my worries release.
Nature's a prankster, but I've got the key,
To laugh at myself—oh, what good company!

Reflections in Nature's Kaleidoscope

Leaves dance like clowns in the breeze,
Chasing shadows with the greatest of ease.
The sun giggles, tickling the ground,
While colors swirl, spinning round and round.

A sneaky vine tries to steal the show,
Waving at passersby, 'Hey! Look at me go!'
With a twist and a twirl, it claims its space,
In this leafy carnival, a wild embrace.

Roses roll their eyes at the joke of the day,
While daisies yell, 'Hey, come join the play!'
The grass whispers secrets, green as can be,
A raucous affair in nature's decree.

Roots stretch like tired limbs, so polite,
As if to say, 'Let's nap 'neath the light.'
With laughter and cheer, the garden hums,
In this vibrant world, joy surely comes.

The Silent Companion on a Sunny Day

A pot of green sits alone on the sill,
Watching the world with a heart full of thrill.
It's soaking up rays, having fun at its post,
While birds chirp gossip about the next roast.

The sunlight pinches its leafy attire,
'Time for a stretch,' it whispers, 'Don't tire!'
With each pop and twist, it claims the warm glow,
Feeling quite grand in its leafy show.

Bee buddies buzz with an eager intent,
Having a tea party, totally bent!
While flowers sway, grooving to the beat,
Our green friend chuckles, tapping its feet.

And though it sits still, with quite the flair,
In a garden of humor, there's joy everywhere.
Its silent laugh echoes, though not a word spoken,
In nature's embrace, all worries are broken.

Curvature of Foliage Dreams

Winding upwards, a vine plays peek-a-boo,
With a cheeky grin, it's waving at you.
Each leaf a smile, bending with grace,
In this leafy wonderland, there's quite the space.

Around every corner, a new joke to find,
With petals that flutter, beautifully blind.
Like a funhouse mirror, it laughs in delight,
Reflecting the sunshine, oh what a sight!

The branches converse in whispers and sighs,
As squirrels get busy with their nut-collecting lies.
Laughter erupts as a flower trips by,
With roots that tangle, oh my, oh my!

In this garden of giggles, where dreams take flight,
The curves of the leaves dance in pure light.
Each twist tells a story, each turn adds to cheer,
In the world of the green, all's held dear.

Growth Beyond the Grasp of Time

A tiny sprout stretches, dreaming out loud,
'One day, I'll be tall, like that big fluffy cloud!'
With determination, it wriggles and sways,
Longing to grow in the sun's frolicsome rays.

The stones chuckle softly, 'You've got grand plans!'
While ants march in circles, making wise scans.
'What's your hurry, friend? It's all in the game,'
They whisper with mirth, 'Life's blissful and tame.'

With each little storm, the sprout bends with glee,
Singing a song, a green jubilee.
As clouds roll in, it embraces the rain,
Swaying like a dancer, unburdened by pain.

In the end, it grows strong and wide,
With roots that hold memories tucked inside.
Each leaf tells a tale of laughter and cheer,
In this journey of green, there's nothing to fear.

A Leafy Odyssey

In a jungle of couch and chair,
The plant has taken its lair.
With a twist and a turn, oh so spry,
It scales the walls, reaching up high.

Sneaking through the kitchen light,
Pothos prowls with sheer delight.
It tags the fridge like a long-lost friend,
Where will it roam, when will it end?

Each leaf a sailor, bold and grand,
Navigating through this plant-filled land.
With pots that promise, but don't quite keep,
Lurking around, never falls asleep.

So here's to the vine with a mischievous grin,
Taking over houses, it's a wild spin.
Just don't forget, as it climbs away,
To water it now, don't make it sway!

Intricate Vines of Thought

Tangled thoughts in leafy strands,
Whisper tales from tiny hands.
Spreading wisdom on the shelf,
Maybe it knows more than yourself.

Each curl a secret, a jest, a quirk,
Could it be helping, or just a perk?
Chasing shadows, the sun's own dance,
A sneaky plant, no second chance!

In this maze of green and grit,
Every day a new misfit.
Conversations with a climbing mate,
Who knew plants could speculate?

With mind and leaf all in a tangle,
Life's not dull, it's quite the jangle.
Grow with laughter, lose that frown,
The vine's got jokes, it's wearing a crown!

The Call of Climbing Kindred

Hey there buddy, what's the deal?
In a pot, do you feel surreal?
Just aim for the ceiling, give it a whirl,
Join the ranks of the climbing world!

With roots like anchors, it's quite the scene,
A gym hall for the leafy green.
Swinging and swaying, no time to stall,
Pothos pals having a ball!

Watch them twirl and pirouette,
On this green stage, they'll never fret.
A family of leaves, so spry and bright,
In a dance-off, they'd win the night!

Here's to the family we love to climb,
Sharing the spotlight, one leaf at a time.
Plant hugs all around, what a fun ride,
In this leafy circus, let's take pride!

In the Wake of Climbing Spirits

Chasing shadows, a leafy dream,
Winding up in a knee-high stream.
With laughter twinkling in each split,
Watch the pothos play its skit.

Like a jester, it weaves through air,
Whispering tales without a care.
It promises leaves with a wink and a nod,
While plotting world domination odd!

In its wake, the mischief flows,
Unruly trails, where nobody goes.
One day they are here, the next they roam,
Befriending shadows, making a home.

So let it climb, let's give it a cheer,
To the wandering vine we hold dear.
In the jungle of life, it takes a stand,
With a wink and a leaf, it's never bland!

Dreaming Under the Leafy Canopy

Beneath the leaves, where shadows play,
I dream of adventures, come what may.
A squirrel darts past, in a suit so neat,
I chuckle and wonder, what's under those feet?

A lizard lounges, sunbathing with glee,
He challenges me to climb that tall tree.
With a gentle gust, he tips his hat,
Frogs join the fun, oh, imagine that!

A dance party starts, under moonlit gleam,
With fireflies twinkling, like stars in a dream.
Hold on to your hats, it's a wild spree,
Even the pillows are laughing with me!

In this leafy kingdom, we're all quite mad,
Each whispering plant, every fruit, is a lad.
A harmony of laughter, both silly and sweet,
Together we'll party, with roots and with feet!

Climbing Towards Tomorrow

I reach for the sky, and my foot's in a knot,
Climbing up branches, I wonder, why not?
A bird laughs loudly, pecking my shoe,
With a wink in his eye, he flies off, adieu!

A sturdy vine sings, with a voice made of green,
It says, "Grab a friend; let's make quite the scene!"
But my buddy is snoring, tucked under a leaf,
I climb on alone, causing comic relief!

A caterpillar grins, he's aiming for flight,
I say, "Hold your horses, you'd spill in mid-flight!"
He chuckles and wiggles, "I'm ready, you see!"
Well, off he goes, and who knew he'd flee?

As I reach for the stars, with mud on my jeans,
I ponder the wisdom of life's little means.
Each stumble a giggle, each slip a delight,
So let's keep on climbing, into the night!

Lush Horizons Await

In a meadow of jokes, the flowers all bloom,
Their petals are laughing, dispelling all gloom.
A dandelion sneezes and spreads seeds of cheer,
While bees do a jig, buzzing close to my ear!

"Hey you with the roots, what's your grand plan?"
I ask a stout fern, who's the wisest it ran.
He chuckles and whispers, "Just sway to the beat,
While wearing your humor as your favorite treat!"

In this merry patch, where the sun's always bright,
All worries grow small, a comical sight.
A butterfly winks as it flits through the air,
"Want to join my cabaret? We'll go anywhere!"

So let's frolic together, through laughter and fun,
With every befriended, sun-soaked, bug-turned run.
The horizon's all plush, and the clouds wear a grin,
With joys yet to find, let the hilarity begin!

Intertwined Destinies

Two vines twist and turn, a playful embrace,
Each fray and each knot, a love-tinged chase.
"Shall we climb to the clouds?" one vine did suggest,
"Sure thing!" grinned the other, "Let's put it to test!"

Together they tangle, with giggles and glee,
As blossoms all blend in a colorful spree.
A bumblebee buzzes, as if to declare,
"Your love's an adventure, worth telling, I swear!"

But roots seem to argue, all tangled and bold,
"Enough with the laughter, we're seeking the gold!"
Yet as they dig deeper, they find hidden jewels,
Network of pals stay, dismissing the rules!

At dusk, the vines laugh, their quest now in sight,
Each twist in the journey a moment of light.
Hand in hand, they sway, in a giggly romance,
Two vines, one heart, in a verdant dance!

The Art of Resilience in Green

A green sprout peeks out with glee,
Dodging raindrops like they're confetti.
Swaying to sounds of a neighbor's cat,
Flexing its leaves, it's quite the acrobat.

In sunlight it basks, a style so bright,
With curls that twist, it's quite a sight.
Tangled in laughter, it takes a bow,
Ready to shine, it says, "Why not now?"

With clumsy vines and a charming grin,
Hurdle the chaos, let the fun begin!
Lost in the weeds, but finds its way,
Turning fails into jokes, come what may.

So here's to greens with sprightly flair,
Chasing the sun, dancing in the air.
A comedian in pots, a leafy delight,
Bringing us joy, morning and night.

Adventures Beneath the Foliage

Down by the roots where the wild things grow,
A troupe of leaves puts on a show.
"Watch me swing!" shouts the fluffy fern,
While the cobwebs nod in delightful turn.

A beetle rides in, with style and flair,
Screaming, "Yikes! Is that a hair!"
Mischief abounds, in the forest of greens,
With bumps and giggles, like silly scenes.

Each leaf has dreams of journeys profound,
Adventure awaits where the soil is found.
They plot and they plan under moonlight's gaze,
Seeking the sunshine in whimsical ways.

So when you gaze down at the vibrant floor,
Remember, laughter is what they adore.
Among the roots and the twirling vines,
Are tales of joy in nature's designs.

Notes from a Leafy Odyssey

A wanderer leaves its pot so bold,
With tales to tell and jokes retold.
"Let's share a laugh," the green sprout cries,
As crickets chirp with curious eyes.

Bouncing through blossoms, dodging the ants,
It winks and says, "Time for a dance!"
A sashaying vine on a trellis high,
Spins tales of love from an old butterfly.

The garden's alive with chatter and cheer,
Creating a buzz that all can hear.
"Hey, seedling buddy, let's make a scene!
Together we'll plot a leafy routine!"

So if you should pause in verdant embrace,
Remember the joy and the silly face.
For laughter is rare, like sun after rain,
Let's water our spirits; let's grow through the pain!

Ascending Through the Canopy

Up in the branches, where giggles reside,
A party of greens is ready to glide.
"Take a chance!" shouts the sprightly vine,
While the old oak chuckles, "It's all divine!"

With each little twist and gentle sway,
The canopy dances, come join the fray!
A fluttering leaf shouts, "Catch me if you can!"
As shadows play tag with a crafty plan.

The sunbeams flicker like playful sprites,
Cheering on petals in their leafy flights.
"Who needs a ladder? We're up here for fun!
With giggles and prances, we'll chase the sun!"

So next time you wander, lift your gaze high,
To see the greens leap, to see them deny.
For in every shadow, and sunlit spree,
Lies the laughter of leaves, forever wild and free.

The Unseen Wilderness

In shadows where we seldom tread,
A funny plant hangs by a thread.
It whispers jokes in leafy sways,
As sunlight dances gleeful rays.

With tendrils stretching wide and long,
It sings a silly, leafy song.
Each leaf a tale, a laugh so bright,
In the unseen, pure delight.

The vines twist round with playful glee,
A jungle gym for sneaky bees.
They buzz along, a comic crew,
At home among the greenish hue.

So next you see a vine that climbs,
Remember here are secret rhymes.
In nature's twist, there's humor spun,
In hidden places, joy's begun.

Depths of Green Wisdom

Beneath the leaves, profound and wise,
Lurks wisdom wrapped in leafy lies.
A plant that chuckles, roots in jest,
In soil-bound riddle, it's the best.

With every curl, a giggle grows,
A sage in green, who surely knows.
It leans on truth, but oh so sly,
"Just water me and I'll comply!"

The nature's jesters twist and twist,
With giggles hum, they can't resist.
For in this green, absurdity blooms,
In wisdom's depths, humor looms.

So join the feast of green delights,
With laughter on those leafy nights.
In each bright shade, the secrets play,
Come sip the wisdom, day by day.

Revelations in the Green Glow

When the dim light catches the leaf,
A revelation sparks with belief.
This verdant glow holds tales of cheer,
In every inch, the magic's near.

With swaying limbs, it does reveal,
The funny truths of life's great deal.
A little twist, a knotty punch,
It leaves us laughing on our lunch.

The glow exposes all that's green,
In shadows where the light is seen.
The quirks of life, in leafy scrolls,
In every line, perfection rolls.

So wander close and heed the glow,
These revelries in green will show.
From herbs to vines, the jokes unwind,
In nature's lap, pure fun you'll find.

Veiled Paths of Discovery

In veils of green where secrets creep,
Lie whimsies where the foliage sleeps.
A twisting vine hides laughter's face,
On hidden trails, it claims its place.

Through tangled leaves and sneaky bends,
With every turn, a joke ascends.
A treasure trove of comic flair,
In nature's arms, a playful dare.

So when you voyage through this maze,
Expect a giggle, expect a craze.
With every step, let laughter grow,
In veiled paths where wonders flow.

Explore the quirks, the twists, the turns,
Where every leaf a lesson churns.
In playful hues of brightened green,
The funny side of life is seen.

Roots Reaching for Tomorrow

In a pot on the sill, they wiggle with glee,
Stretching their tendrils, a dance carefree.
Chasing the sunlight, making shadows play,
Who knew little leaves could brighten the day?

With a sprinkle of water, they wiggle and shout,
"We're thriving, we're diving! What's life all about?"
Tiny attacks of dust bunnies arise,
But they flick them away with a flick of their eyes!

Winding and wrapping, they roam near and far,
Grabbed by a cat, who thinks they're a star.
"Do you think I can climb?" they whisper and grin,
While the pup rolls his eyes, thinking, "How do I win?"

So here's to the greens, their antics on show,
With roots deep in soil and a heart all aglow.
They teach us to stretch, to sway and to bend,
As we laugh with their journeys, our leafy green friends!

Oasis of the Untamed

In a corner so wild, cacti give chase,
While pothos play hide and seek with a vase.
"I'm winning! I'm winning!" the ferns start to shout,
As a rogue spider plant models, strutting about.

With a sip of their sun, they frolic and tease,
Daring the dust bunnies, "Come join us, please!"
A parade of greens in a wonderful spree,
Who knew houseplants could throw a wild jubilee?

On the windowsill stage, they put on a play,
"I'm the queen of the room!" the pothos will say.
The monstera chimes in, "You're merely a vine!"
But they giggle and twist, keeping all things fine.

While laughter erupts through their leafy domain,
An adventure awaits with each cheeky refrain.
In this jungle indoors, they find joy in the dust,
Creating an oasis that's vibrant and just!

A Journey Through Green Halls

On a quest for the sun, little leaves are set free,
Gliding past orchids, scoring a degree.
"What's that over there? A light! It's a dream!"
Squeezed in the window, they giggle and beam.

Sliding past books and a cat in a flop,
In a leisurely race, they wriggle and hop.
"Can you keep it down, I'm napping!" he scowls,
But the pothos just grins, wearing leafy crowns.

Adventurous souls in this green-gloried land,
They wind and they weave, keeping strong, keeping grand.
With stories to share in a playful parade,
As a rubber plant chuckles, feeling quite frayed.

Through the living room halls, they dash and they play,
"We're sprouts of mischief; join us!" they say.
From corners to cabinets, they twist with delight,
Together they flourish, embracing the light!

Flourishing in Forgotten Corners

In shadowy places where dustbunnies lurk,
Pothos thrive bravely, a true bit of perk.
"What's a little neglect? We adore a good hide!"
They giggle and wiggle, finding glee deep inside.

With inches of growth in their leafy retreat,
"We're champions of green! A true botanical feat!"
As they gather in clusters, plotting and scheming,
"What plan shall we hatch? I've been dreaming and beaming!"

A forgotten old pot becomes home to a vine,
"Step aside, old coffee cup! This space is now mine!"
With laughter and banter, they all joke and jest,
Knowing that even the dust must confess.

In corners of whimsy, they twirl and they sway,
Reminders that joy hides where sunlight will play.
For even in shadows, they show us their charm,
Flourishing boldly, they warn us, "Stay calm!"

The Unseen Journey of a Leafy Soul

A tiny leaf began to dream,
Adventurous thoughts, it starts to scheme.
It tiptoed past the garden gate,
Waving at the bugs, oh, what a fate!

It danced upon a sunny breeze,
Tickling branches, teasing trees.
"I'm not just green, I'm wild and free!"
Sang out loud, quite cheerily.

Then came a squirrel, quite a tease,
Balancing treats with utmost ease.
"Hey, little leaf, got room for fun?"
"Just grab a leaf, and we can run!"

At twilight's glow, they spun around,
Creating chaos, lost and found.
In every twist, a giggle burst,
In leafy flight, they'd quench their thirst.

Navigating Shades of Green.

In a world of emerald delight,
A giddy vine took to its flight.
"Where to go?" it surely mused,
"Just a twist and I'll be amused!"

It tangled up in elder's care,
"Excuse me, roots! Please, I need air!"
But the ground was so warm and wide,
"I might just take a leafy glide!"

Towards the sun, it did aspire,
But met a breeze, oh what a choir!
Whirling round with a twist and shout,
"Come along, let's twirl about!"

The shades of green, a playful song,
In every hue where it belongs.
It's not just leaf, but laughter shared,
In winding paths, the joy declared.

Green Tendrils Unraveled

A tendril twisted, quite bemused,
"What's this dance? I'm rather confused!"
With a hop and a skip, it took a chance,
"Let's try this thing, some leafy prance!"

It leaped to where the grass is tall,
And threaded through a garden wall.
"Do I belong here? Or am I lost?"
"Just keep on dancing! Ignore the cost!"

Then a ladybug joined the show,
"With colors bright, we'll steal the glow!"
Together they twirled, a circus bizarre,
Who knew leaves could be such a star?

They laughed with the breeze, a charming delight,
In every twist, they'd rewrite the night.
With each little bounce, the world was a stage,
And leafy souls turned over a new page.

Whispering Vines at Dusk

At dusk, the vines began to weave,
A tale so wild, it made one believe.
"Did you hear the gossip from yonder tree?"
"It seems the flowers are making tea!"

With a rustle and a giggle, they spun around,
Whispering secrets, shared with the ground.
"Tell me more, oh leafy kin!
What joy in petals! Let the party begin!"

They tangled together, a chatty scene,
In shades of twilight, a vibrant green.
"So what if we're sometimes out of place,
Together we'll dance with smiles on our face!"

And under the stars, their laughter soared,
A melody sweet, forever adored.
In wraps of vines, they felt so bold,
Whispers of joy, their stories told.

Green Symphony of the Wild

In a jungle of green where the leaves sway,
Pothos vines dance, leading the way.
A symphony plays on this leafy stage,
Nature's own tune, both wild and sage.

A squirrel in tights starts a ballet,
While frogs croak rhythms, come what may.
The sunbeams wink through the leafy show,
As laughter erupts from the roots below.

With each twist and turn, the fun begins,
A merry troupe of nature's twins.
They slide and glide like they own the place,
In this verdant world, every leaf's a face.

So tiptoe softly, don't disturb their glee,
For laughter echoes through the brilliant spree.
With giggles and wiggles, they charm the land,
In this green symphony, life is grand!

Uncharted Greenery

In a jungle where pots and pixels collide,
The amateur gardener plumes with pride.
With a lighter touch and a hope so vast,
He navigates green, a botanical blast.

"Is this a weed?" he wonders aloud,
As vines tangle up, making him proud.
Cousins of chaos, the sprouts unite,
Creating a jungle by day and by night.

A plant that is stubborn, it turns to the sun,
Yet whispers, "Why not?" when it's having fun.
Sneaking a peek at its neighbor's new spot,
"I'll climb a bit higher!" declares the plot.

So wander these greens, let your worries cease,
In uncharted greenery, find your peace.
A leafy adventure, it's life on a whim,
Where the funny, the weird are never too grim.

Stories of the Serpentine

Twisting and turning, the vine does slink,
It whispers of tales that make you think.
"There once was a leaf that thought it could fly,
But found itself stuck, oh my, oh my!"

With gossip of blooms and a wisdom so sly,
It flirts with the sun, from root to the sky.
"Careful!" it warns, "There's danger above,
But oh, the sweet nectar, it's a treasure trove!"

A party for critters, it's never quite plain,
With bumbles and wiggles and no room for disdain.
The ants wear their hats, the spiders their shoes,
In stories of serpentine, none can refuse.

So follow the twists as each tale unfolds,
In this leafy riddle, life bravely scolds.
With humor entwined in each story shared,
The serpentine sings of a friendship declared.

Life Between the Leaves

Life stretches wide in the leafy confines,
Where laughter is hidden in twirls and vines.
"Look at me!" shouts a curious sprout,
"Life's just a party, come join the rout!"

The roots have a chat, sipping dew from the morn,
While a wiggle-worm wriggles in bright green adorn.
"Did you hear?" they giggle, "Last night's grand tale,
A snail on a skateboard tried not to flail!"

Swinging and swaying, they burst into song,
In this leafy world, you can't go wrong.
They laugh at the spiders who tangle and tiff,
And share tales of fumbles with a cheerier riff.

So come twirl with the ferns and dive in the fun,
In life between leaves, there's joy for everyone.
With greens all around and silliness rife,
Just come on and join this hilarious life!

Glorious Veils of Nature's Peace

In a jungle gym of green,
Leaves twist and play in gleeful sheen,
A vine's tangent makes you grin,
Swinging low, it pulls you in.

Sunlight tickles every leaf,
While squirrels dance, what a belief!
With every rustle, laughter bounces,
In this green world, fun announces.

The snails race at a leisurely pace,
While worms prepare for a slow embrace,
A flower yawns, its petals wide,
As nature giggles by your side.

Oh, this leafy merry-land,
Where branches shake like a comical band,
With each breeze, a quirky song,
In nature's peace, we all belong.

Cymbals of the Wind and Vines

The wind plays tunes on leafy drums,
While vines sway round like playful chums,
Each leaf claps in a joyful cheer,
As whispers drift, the fun is near.

A gust of laughter shakes the ground,
Where vines and breezes twirl around,
With every rustle, jests take flight,
Nature's giggles, pure delight.

Chirping birds join in the riff,
As blossoms sway, they bust a myth,
That in this world, things must be serious,
When all around is simply curious.

Amidst the pranks of wind and leaves,
Even cactus shakes off its thieves,
So dance along and let it shine,
In this wild groove, all's divine.

The Serpent's Journey

A snake in shades of green and gold,
Slithers slick, brave and bold,
With every twist, it laughs aloud,
Wearing nature's quirks like a shroud.

With wiggly moves and goofy flair,
It juggles ferns in the warm sun's glare,
Hissing jokes that flutter by,
As dragonflies buzz and skies fly high.

Each loop it makes is quite the ride,
With critters joining in the slide,
In this serpentine jubilee,
A funny tale is what we see.

So wiggle on, you sneaky sprite,
In this realm of green delight,
With scale and smile, you charm the day,
As nature chuckles in its play.

Tidal Waves of Green Light

A wave of green crashes on the shore,
With tendrils that dance and plants galore,
Each leaf a surfer, riding high,
In this vibrant sea, where laughter's nigh.

Gentle ripples tease a curious pup,
Who skids and spins, just can't keep up,
The bushes roar with girlish glee,
A verdant tide of jubilee.

Laughter floats on the breezy seas,
With each splash, the flowers tease,
Petals shower like confetti bright,
In the fun-filled waves of green light.

So come and dive in, no need to shy,
Join the dance, let your worries fly,
In this tidal wave of nature's cheer,
Where every moment is a reason to hear.

Interlaced Journeys

In a tangle of green, vines twist and shout,
They drag me along, no chance of a rout.
Ferns raise an eyebrow, "What's your next plan?"
I'm just here for fun, not to be a big fan.

Laughter sprouts up from the dirt in the shade,
As I trip over roots that the foliage made.
A wise old pothos, with a chuckle so bright,
Says, "Just keep on moving, it'll all feel just right!"

Chasing the sunlight, I'm feeling quite spry,
But curious leaves let out a mischievous sigh.
"Watch out for the squirrel with the sumptuous treats!"
I'm caught in a dance, while he nibbles on beads.

With each little twist of this green-covered maze,
I discover there's joy in this wild leafy craze.
So here's to the journey, may it grow like a plant,
With humor and laughter, let's frolic and chant!

Serenity in Climbing Shadows

Climbing shadows nap beneath the bright sun,
While vines twist and giggle, it's all in good fun.
"Take your time, dear friend, in this leafy parade,
Life's better with laughter," the pothos conveyed.

A snapshot of greenery, a snap of a vine,
Each leaf a comedian, dancing in line.
"Is this sunlight free? Do you take it in chunks?"
I'm giggling aloud as I dodge all the trunks.

With roots that run deep in a hall of great cheer,
Each vine tells a story that tickles my ear.
"Why did the stem cross the path up ahead?"
"To catch all the sunbeams and dance on the bed!"

Beneath this green laughter, my worries take flight,
As shadows blend freely in the softest twilight.
With each quirky vine, my spirit takes wing,
In a world so absurd, what joy it can bring!

Elegy of the Verdant Heart

In leafy confessions, I find my own wit,
A vine's gentle jibe makes me laugh 'til I sit.
"Tell me," it whispers, with a wink and a sigh,
"Do you think the next petal would ever ask why?"

I ponder the question as I glide through the green,
Where roots are the audience for all that's unseen.
"I think they just bloom for the love of the show,
And maybe for sunlight; they put on a glow!"

The ferns join the laughter, with giggles galore,
As I tumble through shadows that curl on the floor.
"Life's short," says a pothos, "let's dress it with flair,
And twirl through the chaos without any care!"

So here's to the laughter in every bold heart,
As vines weave together, embracing the art.
In this verdant retreat, let humor take hold,
For life's just a joke, let the laughter unfold!

Beneath the Climbing Canopy

Beneath the expansive, leafy green roof,
I'll start my adventure, shake off all the woof.
"Are you lost?" asks the ivy, in cheeky delight,
"Just follow the giggles; you'll find it tonight!"

The dance of the shadows keeps pulling me tight,
As I wander through vines seeking laughter and light.
"Does this path lead to wisdom or just some fine tea?"
The leaves laugh aloud, giving answers to me.

With winks from the flowers and smirks from the air,
My heart takes a leap; what fun is up there?
"Are those hidden blossoms just playing a game?"
"Why, of course!" replied nature, "and you're in the frame!"

In the tangled embrace of this green festivity,
I'm laughing with joy, feeling light as a bee.
For life's just a party beneath foliage high,
Let's dance and enjoy, in the breeze we can fly!

Traces of Hidden Joy

In the corner where vines creep low,
A sneaky sock puts on a show.
Its partner lost, a tragic fate,
Yet here it dances, feeling great.

Laughter echoes through the leaves,
As mischief spins and quietly weaves.
A sneaky squirrel, doing a jig,
Trips on a root, a moment so big.

A gnome with glasses, quite bemused,
Watches the antics, slightly confused.
Whispers of joy flutter in air,
Celebrating all that's oddly rare.

So if you find a pot of gold,
Or a garden gnome's secret told,
Know that there's magic tucked away,
In twisted vines where misfits play.

Fables of Ferns and Fronds

A fern in the corner, proud and spry,
Claims it's the queen, oh my oh my!
While fronds around giggle and sway,
Mocking her crown, they start a play.

A dandelion, brave and bold,
Offers a tale that's seldom told.
"Once I was royal, fit for a king,
But now I'm just fluff, oh the sting!"

The celosia blushes, feels so grand,
Dressed in colors that taste like candy land.
"Let's swap our hats, let's trade our style,
And meet again for a dance in a while!"

Under the moon, they twirl with glee,
A raucous ball of greenery.
Each fable told, a giggle rolls,
Creating history from leafy souls.

Encounters on the Green Avenue

On green avenues where shadows play,
A confused cactus dreams of ballet.
Spinning and twisting, it boldly prances,
While nearby daisies throw him glances.

A rogue rabbit hops, a bouncing fool,
Chasing butterflies down the leafy school.
"Come join my class, we dance at noon!"
But the cacti sigh, "We can't move soon."

A sunflower peeks, gossiping loud,
"Did you see that rabbit? What a crowd!"
But the violets turn, with a roll of their eyes,
"It's just more fluff and foolish lies."

Together they blend in sunlight's embrace,
Finding hilarity in this sweet place.
For even the greenest, oddest of friends,
Can share a laugh until daylight ends.

In the Grasp of Green Whispers

In the garden's hush, secrets unfold,
A whisper from ivy, both shy and bold.
"Did you see that bug with a funny hat?
It thinks it's a bee, but it's really a brat!"

The blossoms giggle, their petals a-flutter,
As a squirrel scoots by, looking for butter.
An acorn on his head starts to sway,
"Look at my crown! I'm king for a day!"

The fronds start to dance, sharing cheeky winks,
While wormy old roots tell the silliest jinks.
"A snail in a race, your pace is too slow!
Just give it a rest, let the garden grow!"

So join in the fun, let your laughter bloom,
In whispers of green, there's always room.
For joy in the garden is never a chore,
It's the heart of nature, forever a roar!

A Dance Among the Leaves

In the corner, green and spry,
A vine twists up, oh my oh my!
It giggles as it climbs and sways,
In leafy dresses, it loves to play.

A frisky waltz with lights aglow,
It leaps and twirls, a grand show!
With every turn, it finds a nook,
As if it's reading a vine-filled book.

Oh, look! A wall becomes a stage,
Our leafy friend is quite the sage.
It climbs and dances without shame,
In the garden, it's earned its fame.

So if you see a vine take flight,
Don't just stare, join in the light!
For in these greens, a jest so bright,
Every leaf's a giggle, pure delight.

Tales of a Vining Wanderer

A sly little wanderer, seeking fame,
It loops and twirls, without a name.
With each turn, it leaves a trail,
Of mischief born on a leafy sail.

It sneaks around the pots at night,
Planning its route, a sly delight.
Oh, what fun to shimmy and slide,
Catching the dirt, like a playful ride.

Each morning brings a new surprise,
Tiny bugs dance in its eyes.
With laughter heard on the sunny floor,
This vining rogue just wants some more!

So heed the tales of this leafy sprite,
With every leaf, it sparks delight.
In pots and nooks, it plays its part,
A wandering soul with a green heart.

In the Embrace of Cascading Greens

Within the room, a green cascade,
A feline friend finds its new shade.
It sways and leans with every breeze,
A dance of greens that aims to please.

Hanging down like ribbons bright,
It teases cats to jump in fright!
"Oh dear!" they say, "What's that above?"
A playful twist, a leaf-filled love.

With curious eyes and twitching tails,
They plot to climb these leafy trails.
But vines just laugh and wave with glee,
"Catch me if you can!" they tease with free.

So join this fun, let laughter bloom,
In tangled greens, there's always room.
For every twist and playful climb,
In nature's jest, we steal some time.

Roots That Reach for Dreams

Deep in the soil, where secrets lie,
A root dreams big, it aims to fly.
"Oh to dance!" it sighs at night,
To reach for stars with all its might.

The tiny tendrils stretch and tug,
Grabbing at hopes, a hearty hug.
With every push, they wiggle free,
"Just let me stretch!" they cry with glee.

While others snooze, this root will scheme,
In its wild world, it's living the dream.
"Just a little more," it whispers low,
"I can almost touch that moonlit glow!"

So here's to roots with lofty goals,
Their silly thoughts bring joy to souls.
In the garden of whims, let's make a scene,
As roots reach out for the wild and green.

www.ingramcontent.com/pod-product-compliance
Lightning Source LLC
Chambersburg PA
CBHW070317120526
44590CB00017B/2722